Welcome to Crich Tramway Village, home of the National Tramway Museum.

When we arrived here in 1959, our site was a typical disused quarry, with spoil heaps, derelict buildings, piles of scrap metal everywhere, and underneath it all, lots and lots of wet, sticky mud! Our first intention was simply to use the space and what remained of the buildings to store and preserve as many redundant tramcars as we could manage to rescue. We soon learned that more people cared about the trams than we had realised. They came to see what we had achieved, and they kept on coming! Before long we found we had created a popular visitor attraction – but that, of course, wasn't the end of the story. More visitors meant more demand for refreshments, souvenirs, toilet facilities… these all had to be provided, and in the meantime, our work on the trams, and on building an appropriate setting for them, continued.

The result is what you see here today, but again, this isn't the end of the story. We continue to develop and improve our museum, to offer new and exciting events, and above all to preserve as many trams and tram-related artefacts as we can. Where appropriate, we restore our trams and display them as they would have appeared during their working life, and, where possible, we return them to operational condition and give our visitors the opportunity to ride on them.

None of this would have been possible without the hard work of many volunteers, staff and Tramway Museum Society members over the years.

Each has brought his or her unique talents, dedication and enthusiasm to the Museum, and each, we hope, has gained a sense of fulfilment, and perhaps also a new skill. Some have been able to improve their CV and their job prospects; others have found an opportunity to attain personal goals, meet new people and make new friends. We are always ready to welcome new recruits to our team.

As a result of our efforts we have received many awards. Our collections are designated as being of National Importance and we received the ultimate reward for our efforts when we became an Accredited Museum. Accreditation is awarded only to museums which meet the exacting standards set by Arts Council England. This doesn't mean we can relax, though, as Accreditation is reviewed on a regular basis. If you see any way in which you think we could improve, please let us know!

We offer a fascinating insight into the history of the tramcar and of the site, incorporating exhibitions, a Woodland Walk and Sculpture Trail, children's play areas, a visit to our shops and a break (or two!) for refreshments.

This Souvenir Guide begins by taking you on a suggested route around the site, providing information about the things you will see. Our staff and volunteers are always ready to answer any questions you may have, and we all hope you will enjoy your day with us.

CRICH QUARRY

As you approached the Admissions building, you no doubt noticed the quarry face ahead of you, with the Sherwood Foresters' Memorial Tower above. This is **Crich Quarry**, which was leased by George Stephenson in 1841. A waggonway carried limestone from the quarry to the limekilns at Ambergate. In 1959, part of the quarry, and its waggonway, was chosen by the Tramway Museum Society (TMS) as the ideal site for storing the tramcars they had saved from the scrapyard.

After passing through the Admissions building, go down the slope towards the tram tracks. **Trams run every 10-15 minutes**, and we aim to have at least three trams operating daily. You can board a tram here, but many of our visitors prefer to begin their visit with a walk to Town End.

Turning left and strolling towards Town End, you will first pass beneath the **Bowes-Lyon Bridge**. This cast-iron structure, which dates from 1844, came from Stagenhoe Park, a stately home in Hertfordshire, and takes its name from the Bowes-Lyon family, who owned another stately home nearby.

If you walk across the tracks when you reach the **'Cross Here'** sign you will see a flight of steps leading to the **Outdoor Play area** and the **Woodland Walk** beyond... but you may prefer to save these until later...

DONCASTER PLAQUE AND THE HORSE TROUGH

Continuing towards Town End you will see, high up on your left, the **Doncaster Tramways Inaugural Plaque**, marking the beginning of Doncaster Corporation Tramways. It was originally sited on the wall of Doncaster's Greyfriars Road depot. If you look across the track you will see the iron-framed windows from the same depot, now installed in the Exhibition Hall.

Next, on your right, is the **Ornate Fountain and Horse Trough**. From 1859 onwards these were a common sight on city streets, and in the days of horse-drawn trams they provided welcome refreshment for horses. Nowadays the trough is home to our fish, and if you are lucky you may see them.

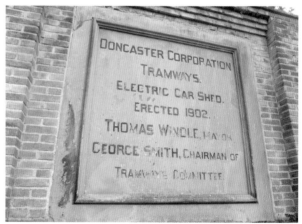

Doncaster Tramways Inaugural Plaque

ALEXANDRA PARK
VIA BRIDGETON CROSS

812

RED LION PUB

The Red Lion originally stood near the church of St Peter ad Vincula in Stoke, otherwise known as Stoke Minster.

There had been an inn on the site since 1818, but when the A500, which passes close to the Minster churchyard, was built in the early 1970s, the Red Lion became the subject of a compulsory purchase order. It was doomed to be demolished, but a reprieve of a kind came along when a new home was found for it here at the Museum.

Originally a hotel, but later ceasing to offer accommodation, the Red Lion had links to Stoke's tramways; the North Staffordshire Tramways Depot was nearby, and it is said that tramway employees sometimes met in the Red Lion to receive their wages. Like other hostelries of the time it was not just a place for drinking, since local functions such as auctions and inquests were also held there. The Tramway Museum, with its trams, street scene, and yearly programme of events and entertainments, was the ideal place for it.

Instead of being wantonly destroyed, the Red Lion was carefully dismantled and its brick and tiled exterior was transported to Crich.

There was quite a delay before reconstruction began, and in the interval the architectural adviser, Jim Soper, transported loads of bricks from Crich to his home in West Yorkshire, where he cleaned and mended them. Meanwhile, the red lion figure which had stood proudly atop the original building waited patiently by the Museum entrance.

Unfortunately the red lion had been accidentally damaged, either when it was removed or in transit, and it was eventually decided that a fibreglass replica would have to stand on the roof of the reconstructed building.

The red lion being lifted into place

The black-leded slate surround to the fireplace in the bar is from the original Red Lion in Stoke and dates from around 1905.

From the Leeds City Tramways Committee Room comes the Poulson Room's mahogany fireplace and brass hearth surround, together with the screen to the cash desk; these are dated 1915, as is the mahogany door at the top of the stairs which comes from the Leeds City Tramways General Manager's Office. Other features, such as the chandeliers and the pitch pine boarding to the bar, were originally sited in churches, while the bar itself comes from the Staff Social Club at Nottingham Prison.

The actual rebuilding was a long process; mostly undertaken by volunteers, it continued throughout the 1990s, and the Red Lion was at last formally opened in 2002.

Ceramic tiles similar to those which adorn the exterior of the Red Lion were once a common sight in Stoke-on-Trent, which is of course the centre of the Potteries district, but we believe this building is a particularly remarkable example. Obviously the tiles made the building look much more interesting and attractive, but they were also cheaper than carved stone and would have been more resistant to discolouration, however smoky the city's chimneys might be.

The 'branded' tiles, like the carved musical instruments on the pediment of the Assembly Rooms, tell the passer-by what can be found inside the building. In the late 1800s and early 1900s it was common for breweries to advertise their products on their pubs, and tiles such as these were an excellent way to do it.

STEPHENSON PLACE

Edwardian Urinal

Beside the Red Lion stands an Edwardian men's **urinal**. This was made by W MacFarlane & Co. Ltd at their Saracen Foundry in Glasgow, and was originally sited at a tram terminus in Reading, Berkshire, in 1903. We don't know if facilities were also provided for women, but in the early days of public conveniences they often were not.

Next, notice the **ornamental ironwork** supporting the verandah at the front of Rita's Tearooms; this came from Ambergate Railway Station, while the railings came from the New Bath Hotel in Matlock Bath.

As you reach Barnett's Sweet Shop you will see on your left a **Stench Pipe**, which in the Victorian age carried hazardous gases away from the underground public toilets and sewer system. This one came from a public convenience near New Street Station in Birmingham. It would once have had a dual function, as a lamp post.

Victorian Stench Pipe

Ornamental Ironwork at Rita's Tearooms

Other historic street furniture items in this area include the Liverpool tram Stop Sign and post. Attached to the post you will also see a red Timetable Case from Sheffield.

The tall, elegant black street lamp near the ice-cream parlour is an example of a City of London Arc Lamp; notice the ornate detail around the base.

Our Penfold Post Box, dating from between 1861 and 1867, is one of five items at the Museum that are Grade 2 listed (of special interest). Our Post Box was originally from Manchester, and you can still use it to send postcards to your friends – there is a daily collection.

Stop Sign

Lamp Post

Manchester Post Box

EAGLE PRESS

The Eagle Press is home to a small printing works, similar to that found in every city and town throughout the land from the early 1800s to the late 1980s, when technology brought about the demise of the ancient and noble art of letterpress printing.

Letterpress printing was invented in 1442 by Johannes Gutenberg at Mainz on the river Rhine. It was introduced to England in 1475 by William Caxton. The process involves assembling letters into words using lead type with all the letters being of equal height (.918"). The type is then inked and paper pressed on top, thus producing a print.

The Eagle Press has a collection of working presses, including a Columbian Newspaper press designed in Philadelphia in 1820.

Our model was built in London in 1859. We also have two Cropper Charlton Peerless presses – built locally at New Basford, Nottingham around 1900 – and a paper-cutting Guillotine from the same era. From the 1950s we have four sizes of Adana table-top models, plus various ancillary equipment.

A large collection of lead and wooden type complements the collection. The Eagle Press produces samples of printing which are available for free.

Beyond the new shelter where parents can leave buggies and prams while they and their children ride the trams, your eye will no doubt be caught by the **Police Box**.

This is a Mark 2 Metropolitan Police Box from London; it is made of concrete and is the only one of its type left in the country. It would have contained a small table and a stool as well as a telephone, so that the 'bobby' could write his notes and report to the police station. Members of the public could also use the telephone to report a crime.

Beyond the Police Box is the **Bundy Clock**, which was used to keep trams running to time. Drivers would insert a key to record their tram's departure. This example is from Birmingham.

Our trams depart from the **Tram Shelter** at Town End, which was in fact a bus shelter from Birmingham. The stained glass, however, is from a tram shelter on the former cable tramway in Matlock.

TOWN END AND GUIDED TOURS

Opposite the Bundy Clock and Police Box you will see a red and white **K1 telephone box**. This type was introduced in 1921; ours is Kiosk number 1, and came from the grounds of a hospital in Rochdale, Lancashire. It contains a historic A & B push-button phone.

Nearby stands a Belliss and Morcom reciprocating **engine and generator set**, which would once have been used to generate electricity to power a tramway system.

K1 Telephone Box

Engine & Generator Set

Guided tours start outside the Assembly Rooms on weekdays at 11.15am and 2.15pm.

Dominating Town End is the façade of Derby's original **Assembly Rooms**. It was built between 1765 and 1774, and was dismantled and brought here after the interior of the building was destroyed by fire in 1963. On the triangular pediment at the top are carved musical instruments which identify it as a place of entertainment – and the instruments actually have strings made of wire.

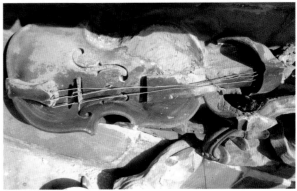

Detail of carved musical instruments

The building originally contained a Ballroom, Supper Room and Card Room, but today you will find two exhibition spaces inside. One houses 'Survive and Thrive: the Electric Era', while temporary exhibitions can be found in the other.

TAKE A TRAM RIDE

You might like to board a tram now, and take a ride to Glory Mine. Look to your left as you travel up the line!

Burnley Corporation Tramway Office

Around the corner from the Assembly Rooms, the Museum's administrative offices and extensive Library are situated behind the frontages of the ***Burnley Corporation Tramways Office*** and the ***Yorkshire Penny Bank*** from Nelson in Lancashire.

The ***Forge Shop***, on your left, has window-frames which date from George Stephenson's time here. The forge itself is preserved inside – look out for it later, when you are browsing in the shop.

Next, as you pass the Red Lion, look left to spot another ***Post Box***, set in the wall at the end of the Depot Fan railings. This is also Victorian, of a style which was in use from 1881 to 1904.

Yorkshire Penny Bank

Post Box

Forge Gift Shop

VICTORIA PARK

Blackpool Stone

As you near the Bowes-Lyon Bridge you will see the **Blackpool and Fleetwood Tramroads commemorative stone** from Bispham tram depot; then, in a niche, is another **drinking fountain**, exclusively for people this time. Donated, like the Tearoom railings, by the New Bath Hotel, it is dated 1873 and features a lion's head and floral decoration. The lion's face was made on-site.

Beyond the bridge is a **K2 telephone box**, successor to the K1. This type was designed by the celebrated architect Sir Giles Gilbert Scott and introduced in 1927.

If you would like to alight at Victoria Park, please let the conductor know – it is a request stop only. The **woodland walk** can be accessed from the road at the side of the park, but we hope you will continue your tram ride, for there is still lots more to see.

K2 Telephone Box

1873 Drinking Fountain

Our **Bandstand** came from Longford Park, Stretford, Manchester, which originally formed the grounds of Longford Hall and was opened to the public in 1912. After the park suffered a decline in popularity during the 1960s, the Bandstand was brought to Crich, where it was restored and given an appropriate setting. On certain days you will be able to see and hear a band playing.

WAKEBRIDGE AND GLORY MINE

The tram will take you to the end of the line at **Glory Mine**, where you can walk to the Sherwood Foresters Regiment Memorial (Crich Stand). Sturdy footwear is advisable for the walk to Memorial.

This is perhaps the most famous landmark in Derbyshire and is situated over 340 metres above sea level.

The Sherwood Foresters (Nottinghamshire and Derbyshire Regiment) was a line infantry regiment of the British Army in existence from 1881 to 1970. In 1970 the regiment was amalgamated with the Worcestershire Regiment to form the Worcestershire and Sherwood Foresters Regiment which in 2007, was amalgamated with the Cheshire Regiment and the Staffordshire Regiment (Prince of Wales's) to form the present Mercian Regiment.

The spiral staircase of the Tower, leads to the viewing gallery from where, on clear days, visitors can pick out 7 counties and various landmarks over the surrounding countryside.

For more information visit:
www.crich-memorial.org.uk

London 159 with Memorial Tower

You may just wish to enjoy the picnic area and watch trams passing by. Returning by tram, you might like to alight at **Wakebridge** to view the Lead Mining display. A visit to the Sub-Station will show you how the electric current is fed to the tramway. If you are keen on recycling, you may also like to take notice of the public toilet by the tram stop.

Here we practice 'vermiculture', which means that the waste is collected in a chamber, where a special variety of worm turns it into compost.

You can now take another tram back to the Village, or return on foot along the **Woodland Walk and Sculpture Trail**.

Some of our sculptures, such as the Wood Ant and the Green Man, are permanent, while others will eventually be reclaimed by the earth, making way for new ones.

The sculptor uses a chainsaw to carve a basic shape from a tree trunk before working on the details. You will see his outdoor studio on your left as you approach the Willow Tunnel, and may be able to see his work in progress.

Sculpture Trail

Derwent View

DERWENT VIEW AND OUTDOOR PLAY AREA

Passing through the Willow Tunnel you will reach Derwent View, where you can picnic if you wish. Then, after negotiating the twists and turns of the **Labyrinth**, turn right along the track until you see a pair of Red Squirrel sculptures. These mark the beginning of the Leaf Trail, where there are a series of posts showing the plants and wildlife which thrive here.

As you continue on your way towards the Village, a wooden walkway on your right will lead you to the the remains of the **Lead Smelter**. Lead has been mined in Derbyshire since Roman times and we are proud to be able to show evidence of an important part of our industrial heritage.

Outdoor Play Area

Next comes the **Outdoor Play Area**, where children can climb, swing, slide, zip and generally enjoy themselves. There are picnic tables here as well.

Descending again to street level by the steps and walking back towards Town End, you will see before you the blue gates, which came to us from Birmingham's fruit and vegetable market and lead to the **Depot Fan**. To the right of these gates is a blue **Police Telephone Post** constructed from parts of three original telephone posts. These Posts were used in Glasgow from as early as 1891, but were only introduced to the streets of London in the late 1920s.

Nearby is a green '**Lucy Box**'. These were so called because many of them, though not all, were made at the Lucy Foundry, Oxford. They contained either a junction or an isolator for the power supply.

Police Post   *Lucy Box*

INDOOR PLAY AREA AND EXHIBITIONS

Passing through the Depot Fan gates you will see on your right the **Indoor Play Area**, which is suitable for children under 10 years of age. (Please note that dogs are not allowed inside).

Next comes the **Great Exhibition Hall**, where the **Century of Trams** exhibition can be viewed. The exhibition takes you on a journey through a century of tramcar development from the horse trams of the 1860s to the last days of the trams in the 1960s.

Great Exhibition Hall

Our **Workshop Viewing Gallery** provides a fascinating insight into the work we do to restore and maintain our collection of historic tramcars. The entrance for the Workshop Viewing Gallery is close to the entrance of the Learning Centre.

Cross the glass walkway from the Workshop Viewing Gallery into our **Stephenson Discovery Centre**, where interactive displays will tell you the early story of the Museum, as well as the reasons why trams were introduced to this country.

Stephenson Discovery Centre

A DAY IN THE LIFE OF YOUR TRAM CREW

As we aim to have three trams carrying passengers on any given day, there are usually nine people on duty to operate and coordinate them – three drivers, three conductors, a relief crew, and the Duty Inspector (DI). All are volunteers.

After they have all signed in to say that they are fit for duty, the day proper begins at 9.30 when the DI briefs the crews about the day ahead. He must tell them about any safety notices and temporary restrictions affecting the running of the trams, and any unusual events or activities. Each conductor also receives a waybill - a sheet of paper on which is written the serial numbers of the tickets he or she has been issued with.

Next comes a decision on which trams will be running. This depends on a lot of things – what's available, anticipated visitor numbers, the weather and what the drivers are licensed to drive. All our drivers must at least have a licence to drive the 'handbrake' cars, a category which includes about half our operational trams; but more driving experience and more training is required before they can drive 'air-brake' trams, or vehicles with unique controls such as Leeds 180 or Sheffield 510. It is the DI's responsibility to ensure an interesting mix of trams, but there is also an element of crew choice, as everyone has her or his favourites – and the opposite!

The trams' equipment and controls are checked and tested, and then one tram travels to Glory Mine to check the line while the others head for Town End. Hopefully the crews will have time for a cup of tea or coffee before the first tram of the day departs.

The driver is responsible for the tram, and its safe operation is paramount. The conductor takes care of the passengers and issues the tickets. In the time it takes to journey to Glory Mine he or she might issue as many as one ticket every 10 seconds! A good driver will pace the journey to help the conductor, and working as a team in this way makes life much easier for both of them. The two-mile round trip to Glory Mine and back takes about 20 minutes, and each crew will complete up to 14 trips during the day.

At lunchtime the relief crew take over each tram in turn so the crews can have their lunch breaks, but if there is no relief crew – remember they are volunteers, and each day we have to rely on enough people offering their services - the trams must be parked up, one by one.

After the last journey of the day the conductor records the number of tickets issued on the waybill, and counts the coins which have been collected. This amount should match the total value of the tickets. He or she then hands the unused tickets and the coins to the DI, who counts the pennies and halfpennies again and checks that everything tallies. Then the trams are driven back to the Depot Fan, where the crews clean the interiors before returning the trams to the Depot for the night.

The crews sign off at about 5.30. It's tiring work, both physically and mentally, but they all agree they derive great happiness and satisfaction from it, and enjoy demonstrating public transport in the early years of the 20th Century to our visitors.

CONSERVATION

Conservation is an ongoing process in any museum, and is extremely important in one like ours, where many of the exhibits are in use, or exposed to the elements year-round.

You may well see conservation work going on as you walk around the Museum; you will certainly see it in progress if you look into the Workshop from the **Viewing Gallery**. We have to maintain, not just the appearance, but also the structural integrity of the objects in our care. We do the work ourselves whenever we can, but at times we have no choice but to employ specialists.

Some of our conservation projects are major ones which may take months, or even years, to complete; others are repeated regularly, or even going on all the time.

Some happen in full view, many others behind the scenes – and many are more complicated than you might expect. For example, we couldn't just give our Police Box a fresh coat of blue paint from the nearest DIY store - we had to find out the exact shade it would have been when it was in use. Samples had to be taken from the Police Box itself and from the Police Post by the Depot gates. Now, as the result of our research, we have not only a Police Box painted its original colour, but also a modern reference number for the correct shade, ready for when it needs another coat of paint in the future.

Naturally the trams in our collection take up a great deal of our time, energy, and expertise. It is not always possible to restore a tram to working order. Some are unique survivals which must be preserved as they are, because they could not be restored without removing, and replacing with new, parts which are in themselves one-of-a-kind historic artefacts. Any decision on how best to treat each tramcar in our collection is taken only after the most detailed enquiry and in-depth deliberation.

The restoration of London County Council (LCC) No. 1 has been an opportunity to carry out an 'archaeological dig'-style investigation of a tramcar. Every stage of the dismantling and rebuilding of this vehicle has been recorded and photographed.

This has revealed many interesting details, illustrating the ups and downs of this tramcar's long working life. Some parts have been stored ready for repair or reuse in the future, others have been conserved; these latter will be used as a pattern when we come to manufacture replacements.

The Workshop Viewing Gallery allows the opportunity to see close up work on parts of our trams you wouldn't normally get to see, such as the trucks and underframes

CONSERVATION BEHIND THE SCENES

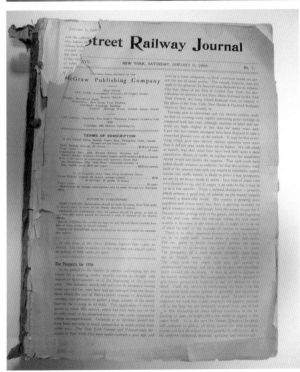

These conservation projects and issues can be seen and appreciated by all our visitors, but elsewhere in the Museum, other aspects of our work are being carried on out of sight. The red door set in the frontage of the Burnley Tramways Office, just across the tram tracks from the Ice Cream Parlour, is the entrance to our Administrative Office, Library, and Archive, and there is much more behind it than you might think.

In the **John Price Memorial Library** we have an extensive collection of tram-related books and journals, over 40,000 postcards and an even greater number of photographs. There are small objects such as badges, buttons and tickets, larger ones such as presentation plates and plaques, and ephemera of all kinds, for example jigsaw puzzles featuring street scenes with trams, and biscuit tins (empty!) shaped and painted to resemble tramcars. We also collect items which relate to the history of the TMS and of our site, together with ones which help to set the trams in context.

Photographs of street scenes or of tramways under construction or repair can give us a wealth of information, while postcards, which may have been given to us solely because of the tram-related photograph on the front, may have a message written on the back which provides useful information for the social historian.

THE TRAMCAR COLLECTION

The Museum is home to the largest preserved collection of tramcars and associated works vehicles in the country. The collection comprises more than 80 vehicles, the majority of which are passenger-carrying tramcars, but we also have several works vehicles, such as tower wagons, water cars/rail grinders and an electric works locomotive for shunting.

Our aim with the collection is to show our visitors the evolution of the tramcar, illustrating each important stage of both technical development and design.

Over 20 different tramway systems and all the leading manufacturers are represented in the collection.

Every year we commission a range of tramcars from our collection, so that visitors can enjoy the experience of riding on an historic tramcar and learn about the fascinating history of each of the vehicles.

Our tramcar collection actually started before the Museum existed, when in 1948 our first tramcar **Southampton Corporation no. 45** was preserved by a group of enthusiasts.

Unfortunately buying a tramcar for preservation was the easy part; the much bigger challenge was finding somewhere to house it. In October 1960, after being stored and displayed in a number of different places, Southampton 45 finally arrived at the Museum, and has held a special place in the collection ever since.

Invoice for Southampton Corporation no.45

CARDIFF 131 & SHEFFIELD 15

In 1959, Cardiff Corporation Tramways 131, our water car, was the first of our tramcars to arrive at Crich, followed by Leeds City Tramways 399 and Sheffield Corporation Tramways 15. Cardiff 131 does actually have a large tank full of water on board, and if the driver accelerates or stops too sharply, anyone on the front or rear platform is likely to get wet!

Horse tram Sheffield 15 became in 1963 the first of our tramcars to operate at Crich.

We had only 200 yards of track for it to run on at that time, but nevertheless it was the first tramcar to carry paying passengers at the Museum. It can still be seen in use on selected days, and for a small extra charge, visitors can take a ride.

40

BERESFORD
SQUARE
VIA KENNINGTON

1622

BLACKPOOL & FLEETWOOD 'RACK' 2

Blackpool & Fleetwood 'Rack' no.2 is one of the oldest electric tramcars in the collection, dating from 1898. The open crossbench style was ideally suited to offer excellent views of the extensive Blackpool coastal scenery when in service.

The tramcar was donated by Blackpool Corporation to the Museum in 1963.

A year later, in 1964, Rack 2 had the honour of becoming the first electric tramcar to run in passenger service at the Museum on the 5th of July.

A popular tramcar in the collection, Rack 2 has covered more than 22,000 miles on our track.

Sheffield Corporation Transport 510 had a relatively short working life, from 1950 until the closure of the Sheffield tramway system in 1960. Along with Sheffield 513 it was decorated for Sheffield's Last Tram Week, after which it was donated to the TMS and brought to Crich, where in 1964 it became one of the first trams to run. Since then it has been an important part of our demonstration fleet, amassing a total of more than 25,000 miles on the track.

The murals you see along the upper deck are not the originals, however. Those unique historic survivals were removed for conservation when the tramcar was overhauled, repaired and renovated in 2012-2014; they were replaced by replicas, lovingly copied by our coach painters.

THE WORKS VEHICLES

Our works vehicles are an important part of the collection, as they not only represent the historical methods of maintaining a tramway and its infrastructure, they also maintain the Museum's tramway.

We could write pages and pages about our trams, from the oldest, Oporto 9, to the youngest, Blackpool Transport Services 762; from London United Tramways 159, with its unusual 'Robinson' staircase, to Croydon Tramlink 058+061, our diesel-powered works vehicle with its hydraulic crane, which links our historic collection with the 'Second Generation' trams of today.

However, we hope you will enjoy riding on our demonstration trams and studying the vehicles on display around the Museum. There are so many more things to discover!

For further details about our fleet, see our website: www.tramway.co.uk

SPECIAL EVENTS

We have a range of events for you to enjoy throughout the year. Each event incorporates the Village scene and Woodland Walk, and, where relevant, the trams from the appropriate era or city of origin are run throughout the day.

Each season, we offer a programme of special events, which add to the spectacle and enjoyment of a visit to Crich Tramway Village. We aim to present a good mix of events - some ever-popular ones may appear each year, while others may be new to our visitors.

The events range from those with an historical theme, such as commemorations of the First and Second World Wars and Edwardian Events, to those with a family focus such as 'Beside the Seaside', bringing the seaside to Derbyshire.

Our 'Beer and Bands' event celebrates local musical talent, while we serve locally-produced cask ales and specialist food.

In the Autumn, 'Starlight Spectacular' sees us open into the early evening. A range of activities is planned for each day, and, after dark, trams run along our specially-lit Village Street.

Owners of vintage vehicles are encouraged to come and display them in the village, and we also hold a couple of vehicle gatherings each season.

For further details about our events, see the 'What's On' section of our website.

What do you need to become a member of the Tramway Museum Society?

Why not be part of our story and become a member?

In 2015 the TMS celebrated its 60th anniversary. During that time we have seen the Museum we founded develop into a major tourist attraction and an internationally recognised research centre for historians, scholars and students.

Our members are just as important to the future of the Museum as they were in the beginning. The Museum's Board of Trustees are all Society members who have been elected to manage the future of the Museum. Ordinary members can attend the AGM and have their say in how the Society is run.

Once you have paid your membership fee, you will be entitled to as many free visits to the Museum as you wish, both when it is open to the public and on special Members' Days.

Various activities are offered on these days, including tram driving taster sessions and behind-the-scenes tours. You can also follow the progress of the Society and the Museum through the quarterly Journal and the Contact newsletter.

Want to join us, or just to find out more?

You can: Fill in a Membership application form on our website, ***www.tramway.co.uk***

VOLUNTEERS

Would you like to join us as a Volunteer?

Volunteers formed The Tramway Museum Society and founded our Museum, and the contribution of volunteers has been vital to its survival and development ever since. Our volunteers carry out a wide range of tasks. They play an important role in the day-to-day running of the museum and are an integral part of its long-term future.

People volunteer for many reasons and in many different ways. Some join us for a couple of days each year, others attend more regularly. Some use volunteering as a way of gaining new skills or improving their job prospects; others simply want to meet new people or to try something new – or maybe they just like trams.

Whatever your reason for wishing to give time to the Museum, your efforts will be much appreciated, and we believe you too can benefit from becoming part of our Tramway Community.

For volunteers who need to stay overnight, accommodation is available in Sam Harrison House, our modern, purpose-built 'home from home'.

Want to join us, or just to find out more?

*You can: Fill in a Volunteer enquiry form on our website, **www.tramway.co.uk**; Email us at volunteering@tramway.co.uk; or Telephone us on **01773 854321**. You don't have to be a member of the The Tramway Museum Society to become a volunteer.*

Would you like to make a donation, to help us continue our work?

All contributions, whether large or small, are extremely gratefully received.

You can: Donate via your mobile phone by texting **TRAM45 £10** to **70070**. To donate another sum, simply replace the £10 in the example with any amount from £1. For more details on how this works, please visit **www.justgiving.com**

Or to specify where you wish your donation to be used, visit our website:

Tram Conservation

www.tramway.co.uk/contact/make-a-donation/

Cash donations can be made using the donations boxes in the Assembly Rooms and Great Exhibition Hall.

ULTIMATE TRAM DRIVING EXPERIENCE

Be a Tram Driver for a day! Master the art of driving vintage trams with expert tuition and leave with a new skill and some great memories.

The day includes vintage tram driving theory and practice, morning and afternoon refreshments and lunch for you and a guest. Other guests are welcome to join you at standard entrance prices and additional costs for their food and refreshments.

If you are over 17 years of age, eligible to apply for a UK vehicle licence, are physically fit and able to carry out instructions safely, please contact us for more details. Gift vouchers are available.

We can also offer a 'taster' Ultimate Tram Driving Experience for corporate groups (maximum 15 people).

For a memorable corporate function, why not consider holding your next meeting, AGM or seminar at Crich Tramway Village with free parking for your delegates?

Meeting room facilities are available, when not used for special events, in either our Poulson Room, suitable for up to 60 theatre-style, or in our Learning Centre, which can seat 38 on tiered benches.

We also have a 14m x 6m marquee, situated next to our Victorian Bandstand, available for private hire for meetings, small exhibitions, wedding receptions and family celebrations.

Your guests can combine the meeting or celebration with vintage tram rides and can enjoy our exhibitions and Woodland Walk and Sculpture Trail.

WHERE TO EAT, DRINK & SHOP

Rita's Tea Rooms

Red Lion Bar

Rita's Tea Rooms – for hot meals (including vegetarian and gluten-free options), sandwiches, delicious cakes, and a range of hot and cold drinks.

Ice-Cream and Refreshments – for a range of locally sourced ice-cream and hot drinks.

The Red Lion – For a selection of local cask ales and cider, local wine, bottled beers and lagers, gluten-free beers, alcohol-free beers, tea, coffee and soft drinks. Pork pies, sandwiches, filled rolls and hot paninis are also available.

The Forge Gift shop – for a selection of gifts, some locally produced. Treat yourself to a memento of your visit!

You can also find a set of the original bellows on display, which would have been used at the original old Forge. They were rescued from the early site by a villager from Crich and offered to Derby Museum. They were then returned to Crich Tramway Village.

You can also purchase a selection of our souvenirs online at www.tramway.co.uk

Barnett's Sweet Shop – for a range of traditional confectionery. It's a nostalgic trip back in time! Some reduced sugar options are available.

Local ingredients are used wherever possible.

TIMELINE

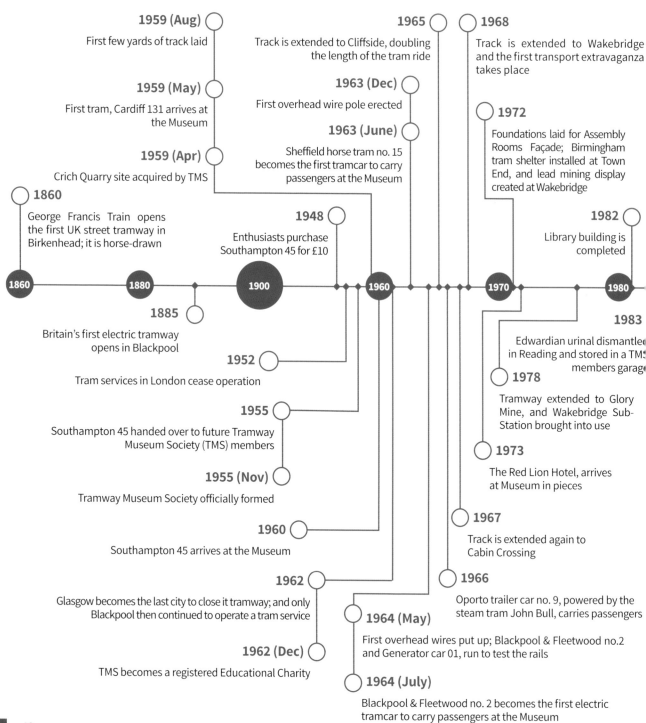

1959 (Aug)
First few yards of track laid

1965
Track is extended to Cliffside, doubling the length of the tram ride

1968
Track is extended to Wakebridge and the first transport extravaganza takes place

1959 (May)
First tram, Cardiff 131 arrives at the Museum

1963 (Dec)
First overhead wire pole erected

1959 (Apr)
Crich Quarry site acquired by TMS

1963 (June)
Sheffield horse tram no. 15 becomes the first tramcar to carry passengers at the Museum

1972
Foundations laid for Assembly Rooms Façade; Birmingham tram shelter installed at Town End, and lead mining display created at Wakebridge

1860
George Francis Train opens the first UK street tramway in Birkenhead; it is horse-drawn

1948
Enthusiasts purchase Southampton 45 for £10

1982
Library building is completed

1885
Britain's first electric tramway opens in Blackpool

1952
Tram services in London cease operation

1983
Edwardian urinal dismantled in Reading and stored in a TMS members garage

1955
Southampton 45 handed over to future Tramway Museum Society (TMS) members

1978
Tramway extended to Glory Mine, and Wakebridge Sub-Station brought into use

1955 (Nov)
Tramway Museum Society officially formed

1973
The Red Lion Hotel, arrives at Museum in pieces

1960
Southampton 45 arrives at the Museum

1967
Track is extended again to Cabin Crossing

1962
Glasgow becomes the last city to close it tramway; and only Blackpool then continued to operate a tram service

1966
Oporto trailer car no. 9, powered by the steam tram John Bull, carries passengers

1964 (May)
First overhead wires put up; Blackpool & Fleetwood no.2 and Generator car 01, run to test the rails

1962 (Dec)
TMS becomes a registered Educational Charity

1964 (July)
Blackpool & Fleetwood no. 2 becomes the first electric tramcar to carry passengers at the Museum

Timeline axis: 1860 · 1880 · 1900 · 1960 · 1970 · 1980

TIMELINE

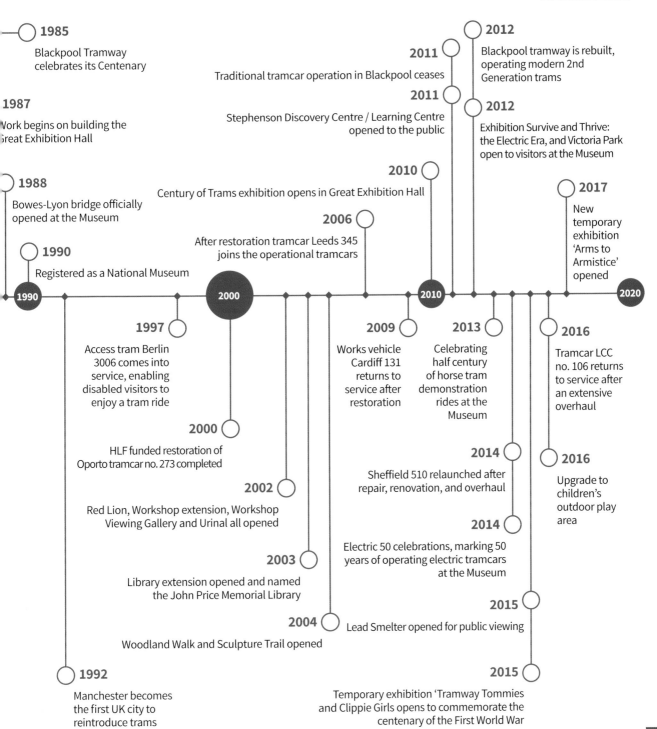

1985
Blackpool Tramway celebrates its Centenary

1987
Work begins on building the Great Exhibition Hall

1988
Bowes-Lyon bridge officially opened at the Museum

1990
Registered as a National Museum

1990

1997
Access tram Berlin 3006 comes into service, enabling disabled visitors to enjoy a tram ride

2000
HLF funded restoration of Oporto tramcar no. 273 completed

2000

2002
Red Lion, Workshop extension, Workshop Viewing Gallery and Urinal all opened

2003
Library extension opened and named the John Price Memorial Library

2004
Woodland Walk and Sculpture Trail opened

1992
Manchester becomes the first UK city to reintroduce trams

2006
After restoration tramcar Leeds 345 joins the operational tramcars

2010
Century of Trams exhibition opens in Great Exhibition Hall

2011
Traditional tramcar operation in Blackpool ceases

2011
Stephenson Discovery Centre / Learning Centre opened to the public

2009
Works vehicle Cardiff 131 returns to service after restoration

2013
Celebrating half century of horse tram demonstration rides at the Museum

2010

2014
Sheffield 510 relaunched after repair, renovation, and overhaul

2014
Electric 50 celebrations, marking 50 years of operating electric tramcars at the Museum

2015
Lead Smelter opened for public viewing

2015
Temporary exhibition 'Tramway Tommies and Clippie Girls opens to commemorate the centenary of the First World War

2012
Blackpool tramway is rebuilt, operating modern 2nd Generation trams

2012
Exhibition Survive and Thrive: the Electric Era, and Victoria Park open to visitors at the Museum

2017
New temporary exhibition 'Arms to Armistice' opened

2020

2016
Tramcar LCC no. 106 returns to service after an extensive overhaul

2016
Upgrade to children's outdoor play area

ACKNOWLEDGEMENTS

With grateful thanks to many of our staff and volunteers for contributions to this guide.

Contributions: Sam Allen; Jan Barratt; Amanda Blair; Gordon Burch; David Frodsham; Roger Michael; Lynn Wagstaff and Laura Waters.

Photographs: Gordon Burch; John Huddlestone; John A Smith; Tim and Sue Stanger; Gill Ward and Malcolm Wright.

Archive photographs: Courtesy of the National Tramway Museum Library.

Editing: Geoffrey Claydon; Colin Heaton; Lynn Wagstaff; Laura Waters.

Our thanks also go to all individuals and organisations involved in donating the artefacts featured in this guide.

And finally, our continued thanks and appreciation to our staff and volunteers who help restore, maintain and present the artefacts and facilities or deliver a service for the enjoyment of our visitors.